Emotional Regulation

for

Adults with Autism

A Comprehensive Guide to Managing Relationships, Reducing Anxiety, and Thriving on the Spectrum

Isabella Wells

© **2024 by Isabella Wells**

All rights reserved. No part of this book may be reproduced or transmitted in any form or by any means, electronic or mechanical, including photocopying, recording, or by any information storage and retrieval system, without written permission from the author, except for the inclusion of brief quotations in a critical review.

Dear Reader,

As a therapist specializing in autism, I've witnessed the transformative power of emotional regulation in countless lives. This book distills over two decades of experience into practical, compassionate guidance for adults on the spectrum. Drawing from evidence-based techniques and real-life success stories, I aim to empower you with tools to navigate emotions, reduce stress, and enhance your quality of life. Join me on this journey of self-discovery and growth - your path to emotional balance begins here.

Warm Regards,

Isabella Wells

Contents

Introduction   9

Chapter One   13

Introduction to Emotional Regulation and Autism   13

    Defining Emotional Regulation in the Context of Autism   13

    The Autism Spectrum and Unique Emotional Experiences   16

    Common Challenges and Strengths in Emotional Regulation for Adults with Autism   19

Chapter Two   25

The Foundations of Emotional Awareness   25

    Developing Self-Awareness and Emotional Literacy   25

    Identifying Personal Emotional Triggers and Patterns   29

    Creating a Personalized Emotion Vocabulary   34

Chapter Three   **41**

Sensory Processing and Emotional Regulation   **41**

    Understanding Sensory Sensitivities in Autism   41

    The Impact of Sensory Experiences on Emotions   46

    Developing Sensory Regulation Strategies   51

Chapter Four   **57**

Cognitive Approaches to Emotion Management   **57**

    Autism-Specific Cognitive Restructuring Techniques   57

    Enhancing Flexibility in Thinking and Emotional Responses   63

    Logical Analysis as an Emotional Regulation Tool   69

Chapter Five   **77**

Physiological Strategies for Emotional Balance   **77**

The Body-Emotion Connection in Autism   77

Autism-Friendly Breathing and Relaxation Techniques   84

Physical Activity and Its Role in Emotion Regulation   90

Chapter Six   99

Mindfulness and Grounding Practices for Autism   99

Adapting Mindfulness for the Autistic Experience   99

Sensory Grounding Exercises   106

Incorporating Special Interests into Mindfulness Practice   113

Chapter Seven   123

Communication and Social-Emotional Strategies   123

Expressing Emotions Effectively in Various Social Contexts   123

Navigating Social Situations and Emotional Challenges   127

Building and Utilizing a Support Network 131

Chapter Eight 135
Managing Intense Emotional Experiences 135

Understanding Meltdowns and Shutdowns 135

Preventive Strategies and Early Intervention Techniques 139

Recovery and Self-Care After Intense Emotional Episodes 144

Chapter Nine 149
Lifestyle Factors for Long-Term Emotional Well-being 149

Creating Autism-Friendly Routines and Structures 149

The Role of Sleep, Nutrition, and Exercise in Emotional Stability 153

Balancing Work, Relationships, and Personal Time 158

Chapter Ten 165
Continuous Growth and Seeking Support 165

Setting Realistic Goals for Emotional Regulation 165

When and How to Seek Professional Support 170

Self-Advocacy and Educating Others About Your Emotional Needs 175

Introduction

Did you know that the average person experiences around 50 to 70 distinct emotional shifts in a single day? For adults with autism, this number can be significantly higher, and the intensity of these emotional experiences is often more pronounced. This startling fact underscores the critical importance of emotional regulation, especially for those on the autism spectrum.

Welcome to "Emotional Regulation for Adults with Autism" – a comprehensive guide designed to navigate the complex landscape of emotions that many adults with autism face daily. As a therapist specializing in autism and emotional well-being, I've witnessed firsthand the transformative power of effective emotional regulation strategies.

I remember working with Alex, a brilliant software engineer in his early 30s. When Alex first came to me, he was on the verge of losing his job due to frequent emotional outbursts at work. His autism had gone undiagnosed until adulthood, and he struggled to understand and manage his intense emotional responses to workplace stressors.

Over the course of several months, we worked together to develop a personalized emotional regulation toolkit. We explored techniques ranging from mindfulness practices to cognitive restructuring, tailoring each approach to align with Alex's unique autistic perspective. Gradually, Alex began to recognize his emotional triggers and implement effective coping strategies.

The turning point came during a high-stress project deadline. Instead of succumbing to overwhelming anxiety, Alex utilized the grounding techniques we had practiced. He communicated his needs clearly to his team and took short, scheduled breaks to manage his sensory input. Not only did Alex complete the project successfully, but his improved emotional regulation skills also led to better relationships with his colleagues.

Alex's journey is just one of many stories that highlight the profound impact of emotional regulation skills on the lives of adults with autism. It's not about suppressing emotions or masking autistic traits; rather, it's about understanding, accepting, and effectively managing one's emotional landscape.

In this book, we'll go into the nuances of emotional experiences unique to adults with autism. We'll explore evidence-based strategies for identifying emotions, managing sensory sensitivities, navigating social situations, and developing resilience. From creating autism-friendly routines to building a supportive network, each chapter offers practical, actionable advice tailored to the autistic experience.

Whether you're an adult with autism seeking to enhance your emotional well-being, a loved one looking to offer support, or a professional working with autistic individuals, this book provides a roadmap for navigating the complex terrain of emotions. It's a journey of self-discovery, growth, and empowerment.

As we continue on our investigation of emotional regulation, remember that every individual's experience with autism is unique. The methods and ideas offered in this book are not one-size-fits-all answers, but rather a diversified toolset from which you can select and customize the most applicable tools for your personal journey.

Let's begin this transforming journey together, harnessing the power of emotional regulation to better the lives of adults with autism. Your path to improved emotional balance and fulfillment starts here.

Chapter One

Introduction to Emotional Regulation and Autism

Defining Emotional Regulation in the Context of Autism

Emotional regulation refers to the ability to regulate and respond to an emotional experience in a way that is socially acceptable and sufficiently flexible to allow spontaneous reactions as well as the ability to defer spontaneous reactions as needed. For adults with autism, this process can be uniquely complex and nuanced.

In the case of autism, emotional regulation entails a complicated interplay between neurological abnormalities, sensory sensitivities, and social awareness. The autistic brain typically interprets emotional information differently, which can lead to more intense or seemingly exaggerated emotional responses. This is not a deficit, but rather a difference in neural circuitry that demands specific tactics and understanding.

For those on the autism spectrum, emotional control could involve:

1. Recognizing and categorizing emotions: This might be particularly complex for autistic individuals who may exhibit alexithymia, a difficulty in identifying and describing emotions.

2. Understanding the intensity of emotions: Autistic individuals may experience emotions more deeply or in a way that feels overpowering.

3. Modulating emotional responses: This entails altering the strength or duration of an emotional experience to meet the current situation.

4. Expressing emotions appropriately: Finding proper ways to communicate emotional states, which may differ from neurotypical expectations.

5. Recovering from emotional experiences: Developing techniques to return to a baseline condition following severe emotional episodes.

It's crucial to note that emotional regulation in autism is not about suppressing or masking genuine emotions to appear "normal." Instead, it's about developing a toolbox of strategies that allow autistic individuals to navigate their emotional landscape in a way that promotes well-being and effective interaction with the world around them.

Understanding emotional regulation in the context of autism also includes knowing that what works for neurotypical individuals may not be helpful for those on the spectrum. Autistic individuals may need to build unique, individualized techniques that correspond with their specific sensory needs, special interests, and cognitive processes.

The Autism Spectrum and Unique Emotional Experiences

The autism spectrum comprises a wide range of experiences and presentations, and this diversity applies to emotional experiences as well. While every autistic person is unique, there are some general characteristics in how emotions are experienced and expressed across the spectrum.

One major feature of autistic emotional experiences is intensity. Many individuals on the spectrum report feeling emotions more intensely and vividly than their neurotypical peers. This intensity may be both a strength and a challenge. On one hand, it can lead to a rich inner emotional life and strong empathy for others. On the other hand, it can occasionally result in emotional overwhelm or difficulty in situations that require swift emotional adjustments.

Another unique characteristic is the experience of alexithymia, which is more common in autistic individuals. Alexithymia entails difficulties detecting and explaining one's feelings. An autistic person could feel a powerful physiological response yet struggle to define the emotion they're experiencing. This can lead to confusion and frustration, both for the individual and for those around them.

Autistic individuals typically feel emotions in ways that are intimately related to their sensory experiences. For example, certain textures, sounds, or visual stimuli could stimulate distinct emotional reactions. This sensory-emotional relationship can be both a source of delight (when connected to special interests or favored sensory experiences) and distress (when linked to sensory overload).

The concept of "special interests" in autism also plays a crucial role in emotional experiences. These deep, focused interests can be a source of considerable joy, comfort, and emotional regulation. Engaging with a unique passion might assist an autistic individual in relaxing when anxious or boost their mood when feeling low.

Emotional experiences in autism can also be characterized by a predisposition for logical or systematic approaches to emotions. Many autistic individuals report evaluating their feelings in a comprehensive, even scientific manner. This analytical approach can be a strength in understanding and managing emotions over time.

It's crucial to recognize that autistic individuals may express emotions differently than what is normally expected. For instance, an autistic individual could not show usual facial expressions or body language when experiencing an emotion, leading to potential misunderstandings in social interactions.

Understanding these distinct emotional experiences is vital for establishing successful emotional regulation strategies that work with, rather than against, the autistic neurotype.

Common Challenges and Strengths in Emotional Regulation for Adults with Autism

Adults with autism confront a unique set of obstacles when it comes to emotional regulation, but they also possess natural strengths that can be exploited to create successful coping methods.

Challenges:

1. Sensory Overload: Many autistic adults are highly sensitive to sensory input, which can easily lead to emotional overwhelm. Bright lights, loud noises, or specific textures can generate intense emotional responses that may be difficult to moderate.

2. Social Interpretation: Difficulty in reading social cues and understanding unwritten social conventions can lead to misinterpretations and unanticipated emotional reactions in social circumstances.

3. Unexpected Changes: Many autistic individuals thrive on routine and predictability. Unexpected shifts might generate worry or tension, straining emotional regulation skills.

4. Communication Barriers: Expressing emotions vocally may be tough, leading to frustration and potential misunderstandings with others.

5. Executive Function Difficulties: Problems with planning, organizing, and shifting focus can impair the capacity to adopt emotional management measures effectively.

6. Co-occurring issues: Many autistic individuals also have anxiety, depression, or other mental health issues that can disrupt emotional regulation.

7. Masking and Burnout: The effort of striving to look "neurotypical" in social interactions (masking) can lead to emotional tiredness and burnout.

Strengths:

1. Intense Focus: The ability to focus deeply on issues of interest can be channeled toward learning and executing emotional management strategies efficiently.

2. Pattern Recognition: Many autistic individuals excel at recognizing patterns, which can be applied

to understanding emotional triggers and successful coping mechanisms.

3. Logical Thinking: A tendency for logical ways can be advantageous in understanding emotions and establishing structured regulating techniques.

4. Honesty and Directness: The predisposition towards plain communication can lead to more honest emotional displays and clearer communication of requirements.

5. profound Empathy: Many autistic individuals describe feeling profound empathy, which can generate strong bonds and mutual understanding when adequately articulated.

6. Unique Perspectives: The autistic brain's unusual wiring often leads to innovative ways of thinking about and approaching emotional issues.

7. Resilience: Having navigated a world not always built for their neurotype, many autistic adults have developed great resilience and problem-solving skills.

8. Attention to Detail: This quality might be beneficial in self-monitoring emotional states and executing comprehensive regulation measures.

The key to good emotional regulation for adults with autism resides in recognizing and dealing with these problems and capabilities. Strategies should be personalized to the individual, taking into consideration their particular sensory profile, special interests, and cognitive style.

For instance, an autistic adult might construct a sophisticated, rational system for detecting and responding to distinct emotional states. They might utilize their pattern identification skills to identify emotional triggers and make disciplined plans for overcoming unpleasant situations. Special interests might be integrated as soothing techniques or rewards in emotional control procedures.

It's also vital to create circumstances that assist emotional regulation. This could require modifying sensory inputs, establishing clear routines, and educating others about autism communication styles and demands.

By embracing both the problems and strengths associated with autism, adults on the spectrum can build tailored, successful ways to emotional regulation that promote their overall well-being and quality of life.

Chapter Two

The Foundations of Emotional Awareness

Developing Self-Awareness and Emotional Literacy

Developing self-awareness and emotional literacy is a vital first step in mastering emotional regulation for adults with autism. This process entails learning to notice, understand, and communicate one's emotional states, as well as understanding how these emotions influence thoughts and behaviors.

For many autistic individuals, this might be particularly tough due to alexithymia, a condition characterized by difficulties identifying and describing emotions. However, with practice and the correct tools, it's possible to greatly develop emotional self-awareness.

One successful way is to start with physical sensations. Emotions typically appear in the body before we consciously notice them. For instance, fear could create a constriction in the chest, while excitement could contribute to a fluttery feeling in the stomach. By paying close attention to these physical clues, autistic individuals can begin to correlate bodily sensations with emotional experiences.

Creating a 'body map' might be a valuable visual tool. This entails drawing an outline of a human body and color-coding different sections based on where various emotions are felt. Over practice, this can help in quickly distinguishing emotions based on physical sensations.

Another key part of growing emotional literacy is learning to discern between different intensity levels of emotions. For example, identifying the difference between feeling somewhat bothered, frustrated, and enraged. A handy tool for this is the emotion thermometer, where different levels of emotional intensity are mapped onto a thermometer-like scale.

Mindfulness activities can also be highly beneficial. Regular mindfulness activities train the brain to observe thoughts and sensations without quick judgment or reaction. This can help in gaining a more nuanced knowledge of one's emotional world. For autistic individuals, mindfulness techniques might need to be customized to suit their sensory preferences and cognitive style.

Journaling is another powerful method for improving emotional self-awareness. Regular meditation on daily experiences and the feelings they elicit might uncover patterns and deepen understanding over time. For those who like structure, employing prompts or pre-formatted notebook pages can be useful.

It's vital to stress that increasing emotional literacy is not about changing or repressing feelings, but rather about understanding them better. This understanding sets the foundation for effective emotional management measures.

For autistic adults, it can be helpful to treat emotional literacy as a unique interest or area of study. Treating emotions as a subject to be analyzed and understood might exploit the autistic qualities of intense focus and systematic reasoning.

Lastly, growing emotional literacy also requires understanding the emotions of others. While this can be tough for many autistic folks, it's a crucial ability for navigating social settings and relationships. Practicing understanding facial expressions, body language, and tone of voice can be helpful. However, it's equally vital to acknowledge that autistic folks may express emotions differently, and that's okay.

Remember, growing self-awareness and emotional literacy is a gradual process. It demands patience, practice, and self-compassion. Celebrating little triumphs along the road can help retain motivation and encourage progress.

Identifying Personal Emotional Triggers and Patterns

Identifying personal emotional triggers and patterns is a vital step in building effective emotional management tactics. For individuals with autism, this process can be both demanding and instructive, affording vital insights into their particular emotional terrain.

Emotional triggers are certain situations, events, or stimuli that consistently provoke powerful emotional responses. These can be environmental (such as loud noises or crowded settings) or internal (such as particular thoughts or memories). Patterns, on the other hand, refer to recurring emotional reactions or behaviors that occur in response to certain triggers.

One effective technique to start discovering triggers and trends is through rigorous observation and documentation. This corresponds well with the detail-oriented temperament of many autistic folks. Keeping a detailed emotional record can be immensely useful. **This log should include:**

1. The situation or incident
2. The emotion experienced
3. The strength of the feeling (on a scale of 1-10)
4. Physical sensations related to the emotion
5. Thoughts that accompanied the mood
6. Behaviors or behaviors conducted in reaction

Over time, patterns will start to develop from this data. For instance, you could find that you constantly feel uneasy in crowded areas, or that certain types of social interactions lead to feelings of frustration.

It's crucial to pay attention to both negative and positive stimuli. While we generally focus on what causes discomfort, understanding what consistently offers joy, peace, or excitement can be equally valuable for emotional regulation.

For many autistic individuals, sensory triggers play a key role in emotional experiences. Conducting a comprehensive sensory audit might be useful. This involves methodically examining your reactions to different sensory inputs (sounds, lighting, textures, smells, etc.) and how they affect your emotional state.

Another beneficial technique is the ABC (Antecedent-Behavior-Consequence) analysis, often used in cognitive behavioral therapy. **This includes dividing down emotional events into:**

- Antecedent: What happened just before the emotional response?
- Behavior: What was the emotional response and associated behaviors?
- Consequence: What happened as a result of the emotional response?

This study can uncover trends in what generates emotions and how these feelings affect your life.

It's also vital to analyze the role of masking or camouflaging in emotional patterns. Many autistic adults devote tremendous work to striving to appear "neurotypical" in social circumstances. This masking can itself be an emotional trigger, often leading to tiredness and burnout.

Understanding your thresholds is another key factor. This includes knowing at what point particular experiences (such as social engagement or sensory input) move from bearable to overpowering. Keeping note of these thresholds can aid in preemptively controlling potential emotional excess.

Remember that triggers and patterns might vary over time. Regular review is crucial. What was previously a huge trigger could become more manageable with practice, while new triggers may emerge as life circumstances change.

Lastly, it's crucial to approach this process with self-compassion and without judgment. The goal is not to eliminate all emotional triggers (which is neither possible nor desirable) but to understand them better. This understanding is the foundation for developing personalized coping methods and creating surroundings that encourage emotional well-being.

By rigorously analyzing personal emotional triggers and patterns, persons with autism can acquire significant insights into their emotional experiences. This understanding forms the basis for building focused, successful emotional control measures that work with their neurology rather than against it.

Creating a Personalized Emotion Vocabulary

Creating a tailored emotion language is a strong technique for boosting emotional awareness and management, especially for persons with autism who may struggle with traditional ways of defining feelings. This process entails building a unique set of words, phrases, or even metaphors that effectively reflect your emotional experiences.

The idea is not to conform to conventional emotion classifications, but to create ways of articulating emotions that resonate with your particular experiences and communication style. This personalized vocabulary can act as a bridge between your internal emotional world and your capacity to articulate these feelings to others.

To begin constructing your emotional language, start by reflecting on your emotional experiences. Consider occasions when you've felt intense emotions, both pleasant and negative. How would you express these feelings in your own words? What pictures or sensations come to mind?

For many autistic individuals, emotions could be experienced more as bodily sensations or visual images rather than abstract feelings. Your personalized vocabulary might contain expressions like "my chest feels like it's filled with buzzing bees" to represent fear, or "my mind feels like a sunlit meadow" to describe contentment.

Special interests can be a fantastic source of inspiration for your emotional vocabulary. If you have a deep interest in a certain subject, you could find it simpler to describe feelings using vocabulary from that field. For instance, someone interested in weather might express their feelings in terms of meteorological occurrences — "I'm feeling stormy" or "There's a calm front moving in."

Creating visual representations might also be beneficial. This might involve drawing, painting, or even producing digital art that portrays different emotional emotions. These visual representations can become part of your emotional language, allowing you to point to an image when words are difficult to find.

Another way is to construct a personal emotion scale. Instead of using typical labels like "happy" or "sad," you might use a numerical scale or a series of personally relevant terms to represent different levels of emotional intensity. For example, your scale might vary from "1 - Completely shutdown" to "10 - Sensory overload."

It might also be helpful to construct subgroups for complex emotions. For instance, instead of just "angry," you might have multiple separate phrases that describe different sorts or levels of anger — from moderate irritation to full-blown rage.

Remember that your emotional vocabulary doesn't have to be restricted to single words. Phrases, sentences, or even short stories could better represent your emotional experiences. The trick is to identify descriptions that seem true and meaningful to you.

As you construct your vocabulary, it's crucial to document it in a form that works for you. This might be a written list, a digital document, a series of drawings, or even a personal wiki. Having this information readily available can be immensely helpful when you're trying to identify or convey your feelings.

It's also vital to discuss your particular vocabulary with trustworthy friends, family members, or therapists. This can considerably boost communication regarding your emotional states and requirements. You might even construct a "translation guide" to assist people in comprehending your unique emotional language.

Remember that your emotional vocabulary is not static. It can and should evolve as you gain greater insight into your emotional experiences. Regularly examining and refining your vocabulary can be a beneficial exercise in continuing emotional awareness.

Creating a bespoke emotion language is not only about discovering new ways to name feelings. It's about acquiring a deeper grasp of your emotional environment and empowering yourself to share these experiences effectively. For individuals with autism, this individualized approach to emotional literacy can be a game-changer in controlling emotions and boosting overall well-being.

By embracing your unique style of feeling and describing emotions, you're not just increasing your emotional regulation skills - you're also honoring your neurodivergent viewpoint on the world of emotions.

Chapter Three

Sensory Processing and Emotional Regulation

Understanding Sensory Sensitivities in Autism

Sensory sensitivities are a key component of autism spectrum disorder (ASD) and play a significant role in the emotional experiences of autistic individuals. Understanding these sensitivities is vital for creating successful emotional management strategies.

Sensory processing in autism often differs from neurotypical experiences in various ways. Autistic individuals may be hyper-sensitive (over-responsive) or hypo-sensitive (under-responsive) to certain sensory inputs, or they may experience a combination of both. These sensitivities can affect any or all of the seven sensory systems:

1. Visual (sight)
2. Auditory (hearing)
3. Tactile (touch)
4. Olfactory (smell)
5. Gustatory (taste)
6. Vestibular (balance and spatial orientation)
7. Proprioceptive (body awareness)

Hypersensitivity can make typical sensory inputs feel overpowering or painful. For example, strong lights could be interpreted as blinding, or a mild touch might feel like sandpaper on the skin. On the other side, hyposensitivity could result in a diminished awareness of some sensory inputs, leading to sensory-seeking activities to receive the essential stimulation.

It's crucial to note that sensory sensitivities can alter over time and in different settings. An autistic individual could be hypersensitive to sounds one day and relatively tolerant the next, or they might be oversensitive in strange situations but comfortable in familiar ones.

Sensory processing impairments in autism are hypothesized to be connected to variations in neural connections and information processing in the brain. Research suggests that autistic brains may receive sensory information more intensively and may have difficulties filtering out extraneous sensory stimuli.

Another key part of sensory processing in autism is sensory integration. This refers to the brain's ability to organize and analyze sensory input from several sources simultaneously. Many autistic individuals exhibit issues with sensory integration, which can lead to feelings of overwhelm or bewilderment in sensory-rich surroundings.

Sensory overload is a frequent experience for many autistic persons. This occurs when the amount or intensity of sensory input surpasses the individual's capacity to process it efficiently. Sensory overload can produce significant emotional responses, including anxiety, anger, or shutdowns.

On the flip side, some autistic individuals may display sensory-seeking behaviors. These are actions taken to get additional sensory input, such as spinning, swaying, or touching certain materials repeatedly. These acts typically function as self-regulation mechanisms, helping to relax or energize the individual.

It's vital to remember that sensory experiences in autism are highly individual. What causes discomfort for one individual could be joyful or neutral for another. This customized character of sensory sensitivities underlines the necessity of personalized methods for sensory management and emotional regulation.

Understanding sensory sensitivities also requires identifying their impact on daily living. Sensory problems can limit an autistic adult's ability to work, interact, and engage in self-care tasks. For instance, sensitivity to specific materials could limit wardrobe choices or hearing sensitivities might make it difficult to work in open-plan offices.

Lastly, it's crucial to consider sensory sensitivities not just as problems, but also as potential assets. Many autistic individuals report that their heightened sensory awareness allows them to see subtleties others might miss or to appreciate sensory experiences in unique and meaningful ways.

By establishing a comprehensive awareness of sensory sensitivities in autism, individuals can begin to define their sensory profile and build techniques to regulate their sensory environment efficiently. This concept offers the framework for addressing the complicated interplay between sensory experiences and emotional control in autism.

The Impact of Sensory Experiences on Emotions

The link between sensory experiences and emotions is particularly pronounced in autism, with sensory inputs often having a direct and significant impact on emotional states. Understanding this relationship is key to efficient emotional management.

Sensory encounters can cause a wide range of emotional responses in autistic individuals. For some, certain sensory inputs could create feelings of serenity and joy, while others might provoke worry, wrath, or overwhelm. These emotional responses can be powerful and quick, frequently looking excessive to neurotypical onlookers who may not grasp the sensory basis of the experience.

One of the key ways sensory experiences affect emotions is through the stress response. When an autistic individual meets aversive sensory inputs, it might trigger the body's fight-flight-freeze response. This physiological reaction floods the body with stress chemicals like cortisol and adrenaline, resulting in emotions of worry, irritation, or panic. Over time, continuous exposure to harsh sensory situations can contribute to long-term anxiety and mood disorders.

Conversely, pleasant sensory experiences can have a substantially favorable effect on emotions. Many autistic adults say that some sensory inputs – like specific textures, noises, or visual patterns – can elicit emotions of joy, relaxation, or comfort. These pleasurable sensory experiences can act as useful tools for emotional control and self-soothing.

The impact of sensory encounters on emotions can also be cumulative. Throughout the day, an autistic individual may confront several sensory problems, each adding to their overall stress load. This accumulation of sensory stress can lead to a steady decline in emotional stability, potentially resulting in meltdowns or shutdowns if the individual hits their sensory threshold.

It's vital to highlight that the emotional impact of sensory experiences can be highly context-dependent. A sensory input that's manageable or even delightful in one scenario could become overwhelming in another, depending on factors like exhaustion, stress levels, or the presence of additional sensory stimuli.

The interplay between sensory impressions and emotions can also form feedback loops. For example, concern about prospective sensory discomfort can heighten sensory sensitivity, which in turn raises anxiety. Breaking these loops generally requires addressing both the sensory and emotional components simultaneously.

Another key feature is the significance of interoception - the awareness of the internal state of the body. Many autistic individuals report issues with interoception, which can confound the process of integrating body sensations with emotional feelings. This might make it tough to detect and respond to emotions before they become overwhelming.

The impact of sensory experiences on emotions continues beyond immediate reactions. Chronic sensory problems might influence overall mood and mental health. For instance, persistent difficulty with auditory processing in noisy surroundings could lead to social disengagement and feelings of loneliness.

On the bright side, many autistic adults report that specific sensory experiences associated with their special interests can cause moments of flow and intense happy emotions. Engaging with these preferred sensory inputs can be a valuable tool for emotional regulation and overall well-being.

Understanding the tremendous impact of sensory experiences on emotions is vital for autistic persons and others who support them. It underlines the necessity of building sensory-friendly surroundings and adopting individualized ways to control sensory inputs successfully. By recognizing and addressing the sensory basis of many emotional reactions, autistic individuals can achieve greater control over their emotional lives and general quality of life.

Developing Sensory Regulation Strategies

Developing adequate sensory modulation methods is critical for emotional well-being in autistic adults. These tactics try to produce a balanced sensory diet that fulfills individual demands and helps preserve emotional equilibrium. **Here are numerous techniques for creating and applying sensory control strategies:**

1. Sensory Profiling: The first step in establishing effective tactics is to create a complete sensory profile. This entails rigorously documenting reactions to numerous sensory inputs across all sensory systems. Tools like the Adult/Adolescent Sensory Profile can be helpful, but personal observation and journaling are equally valuable. Note both painful and joyful sensory experiences, as well as their intensity and impact on emotional state.

2. Environmental Modifications: Once you understand your sensory needs, you may begin to alter your environment accordingly. This might involve:

- Using noise-canceling headphones or earplugs in noisy environments

- Adjusting lighting (e.g., utilizing lamps instead of overhead lights)

- Creating a dedicated sensory-friendly place at home or work

- Using weighted blankets or compression gear for proprioceptive input

- Choosing garments made from comfortable fabrics

3. Sensory Breaks: Incorporate regular sensory breaks into your everyday routine. These are short moments dedicated to either soothing overstimulated senses or giving essential sensory stimulation. Examples can include:

- Taking a little walk outside

- Engaging in deep-pressure activities like self-massage
- Using fidget toys or stress balls
- Listening to relaxing music or nature sounds
- Engaging in repetitive, relaxing movements like rocking or spinning

4. Sensory Toolkit: Develop a portable sensory toolkit that you can bring with you. This might include items like:
- Sunglasses for visual sensitivity
- Scented items for olfactory regulation
- Chewelry or gum for oral sensory demands
- Fidget toys for tactile stimulation
- A white noise app on your phone for auditory regulation

5. Sensory Scheduling: Plan your day with your sensory needs in mind. For instance, schedule demanding activities when you're likely to be in a good sensory condition and plan recuperation time following potentially overwhelming situations.

6. Gradual Exposure: For problematic sensory inputs that can't be avoided, consider a gradual exposure method. Slowly raise your tolerance over time in controlled, moderate amounts.

7. Proprioceptive Activities: Engage in activities that give strong proprioceptive input, which can have a soothing and organizing influence on the nervous system. This can include:
- Heavy job activities such as gardening or moving furniture
- Resistance exercises or weightlifting
- Yoga or pilates
- Using a therapeutic ball or trampoline

8. Vestibular Regulation: Activities that stimulate the vestibular system can be useful for some persons. This can include:
- Swinging
- Rocking in a rocking chair
- Spinning (if tolerated)

- Balance exercises

9. Mindfulness Practices: Adapt mindfulness practices to focus on sensory sensations. This can help raise awareness of your sensory state and early indicators of overload.

10. Stim-Friendly Policies: Advocate for acceptance of self-stimulatory behaviors (stimming) in your business and social circles. These activities often serve a crucial sensory regulating role.

11. Professional Support: Consider working with an occupational therapist who specializes in sensory integration. They can provide individualized methods and interventions.

12. Technology Aids: Explore apps and technologies meant to help with sensory regulation, such as biofeedback tools or ambient noise producers.

13. Communication Strategies: Develop clear strategies to communicate your sensory demands to others. This can involve developing a sensory preference card that you can share with friends, family, or colleagues.

Remember, sensory regulating mechanisms are extremely individual. What works for one individual may not work for another. It's crucial to experiment with diverse ways and regularly examine their success. Additionally, sensory needs might alter over time or in different circumstances, thus flexibility and constant self-reflection are crucial.

By adopting a broad set of sensory regulation methods, autistic adults can form a foundation for enhanced emotional regulation and overall well-being. These tactics not only help in controlling stressful sensory experiences but also in creating positive sensory experiences that boost quality of life.

Chapter Four

Cognitive Approaches to Emotion Management

Autism-Specific Cognitive Restructuring Techniques

Cognitive restructuring is a strong strategy for managing emotions by identifying and correcting harmful cognitive processes. For adults with autism, typical cognitive restructuring treatments may need to be changed to correspond with autistic thinking styles and experiences. Here are several autism-specific cognitive restructuring techniques:

1. Concrete Thought Analysis: Many autistic individuals tend to think in concrete rather than abstract terms. Instead of engaging with abstract

emotional concepts, break down thoughts into distinct, tangible components. For example, rather than addressing "anxiety" as a whole, focus on particular worried thoughts like "I will make a mistake during my presentation."

2. Visual Thought Mapping: Create visual representations of thought processes using flowcharts, mind maps, or other diagrams. This can aid in identifying the connections between thoughts, emotions, and behaviors more clearly. For instance, construct a flowchart indicating how a given experience leads to certain thoughts, which in turn lead to emotional responses and behaviors.

3. particular Interest Integration: Incorporate particular interests into the cognitive remodeling process. Use analogies or examples from areas of keen interest to explain and explore emotional topics. For example, if you're interested in astronomy, you might equate regulating emotions to traversing different planetary atmospheres.

4. Systematic Thought confronting: Develop a disciplined, step-by-step procedure for confronting problematic concepts. This could involve constructing a systematic questionnaire or checklist to evaluate the validity of thoughts. Questions could include: "What evidence supports this thought?" "Is there another explanation?" "What would I tell a friend in this situation?"

5. Emotion-Logic Bridges: Many autistic individuals have a strong aptitude for logic. Create connections between emotional experiences and intellectual analysis. For instance, rate the strength of an emotion on a scale of 1-10, then list logical reasons why it might not warrant such a high ranking.

6. Pattern Recognition in Thoughts: Utilize the often-strong pattern recognition skills in autism to discover repeating thought patterns. Create a "thought catalog" where you record and categorize

different types of thoughts, making it simpler to detect and question them in the future.

7. Social Script Reframing: For thinking connected to social interactions, establish alternative social scripts. If you often think "I don't know what to say in conversations," establish a list of go-to questions or subjects that may be used in many social situations.

8. Sensory-Cognitive Links: Recognize how sensory experiences influence ideas and vice versa. Develop techniques to address sensory discomfort that may be fuelling negative thoughts. For example, if bright lighting in a store leads to thoughts of "I can't handle this," the method can involve donning sunglasses and reassuring yourself "With my sunglasses, I can manage this environment."

9. Literal Language Use: When confronting thoughts, use straightforward, literal language. Avoid metaphors or idioms that can be confusing.

Instead of stating "Don't make a mountain out of a molehill," say "Are you giving this problem more importance than it deserves?"

10. Time-Based Thought Analysis: For autistic individuals who struggle with seeing time, use realistic time-based inquiries to test thoughts. For instance, "Will this matter in a day? A week? A year?" This might aid in obtaining perspective on the long-term impact of current worries.

11. Fact-Checking Routines: Establish a routine for fact-checking thoughts against objective evidence. This could involve keeping a log of forecasts and results, or periodically checking reliable sources to verify worry-inducing information.

12. Rule Modification: Many autistic individuals enjoy clear rules. When recognizing problematic thought patterns, portray them as rules that require altering. For example, replace "I must never make

mistakes" with "It's okay to make mistakes sometimes, as long as I learn from them."

13. Technology-Aided Restructuring: Utilize apps or software created for cognitive restructuring, which can provide an organized, interactive approach to challenging concepts. Some apps allow for customization, which can be adapted to autistic preferences.

By modifying cognitive restructuring approaches to correspond with autistic thinking styles, adults with autism can more effectively challenge and modify harmful thought habits. This individualized approach not only makes the process more accessible but also harnesses the specific abilities often associated with autistic cognition, such as attention to detail, pattern recognition, and logical reasoning. As with any cognitive method, continuous practice and customization are important to success.

Enhancing Flexibility in Thinking and Emotional Responses

Enhancing cognitive and emotional flexibility is critical for efficient emotion management, particularly for individuals with autism who may lean towards rigid thinking patterns. Flexibility in this context refers to the ability to modify thoughts and emotional responses to changing conditions, evaluate other views, and move between different cognitive and emotional states. **Here are techniques to promote flexibility in thought and emotional responses:**

1. Cognitive Flexibility Exercises: Engage in activities that promote flexible thinking. This could include solving puzzles with many solutions, playing strategy games, or practicing improvisation activities. For example, the game "Alternate Uses" where you list as many uses as possible for an everyday object can be extremely useful.

2. Perspective-Taking Practice: Regularly practice considering issues from multiple angles. This can be done through systematic exercises, such as evaluating characters in books or movies, or by real-life scenario analysis. Create a "perspective wheel" with different viewpoints to rotate through when examining a scenario.

3. Emotion Scaling: Instead of perceiving emotions in black-and-white terms, practice recognizing and expressing emotions on a continuum. Use a numerical scale (1-10) or a visual spectrum to illustrate varying intensities of emotions. This helps in comprehending that emotions can exist in varied degrees.

4. Flexible Routine adding: While routines can be reassuring, explore adding flexibility into daily routines. Start with minor, planned modifications and gradually raise the level of spontaneity. For

instance, take a different route to work once a week or try a new cuisine item periodically.

5. "What If" Scenarios: Regularly engage in "what if" thinking activities. This entails picturing possible outcomes to circumstances and thinking how you could respond. Create a list of prospective circumstances and practice mentally working through various responses.

6. Cognitive Reappraisal Training: Practice reframing experiences in different ways. When faced with a hard scenario, actively produce multiple interpretations. For example, if someone doesn't answer your message, instead of assuming they're ignoring you, consider other possibilities (they're busy, they haven't seen it, etc.).

7. Emotion Blending: Recognize that multiple emotions can coexist. Practice detecting and accepting seemingly contradicting emotions. Use

tools like emotion wheels to explore the intricacies and combinations of different emotions.

8. Flexibility-Focused Mindfulness: Adapt mindfulness practices to focus on cognitive and emotional flexibility. During meditation, try watching thoughts and emotions without attachment, letting them come and go. This aids in building a more flexible interaction with interior events.

9. Gradual Exposure to Change: Systematically expose yourself to tiny changes in a controlled manner. Create a "flexibility ladder" where you gradually tackle increasingly hard changes, starting from the easiest and working your way up.

10. Flexible Goal Setting: Practice setting objectives with built-in flexibility. Instead of rigid, all-or-nothing objectives, develop goals with several acceptable outcomes. Use "and/or" statements in

goal formulation to allow for different paths to accomplishment.

11. Social Flexibility Training: In social circumstances, develop flexible conversation techniques. This can involve drafting a list of different responses to frequent social settings or practicing transitioning conversation topics smoothly.

12. Emotion Regulation Variety: Develop a wide toolset of emotion regulation tactics. Practice employing several tactics in varied situations to avoid over-reliance on a single approach. Create an "emotion regulation menu" to choose from in different scenarios.

13. Cognitive Defusion Strategies: Learn and practice cognitive defusion strategies from Acceptance and Commitment Therapy (ACT). These approaches help in building distance from thoughts, making it easier to shift perspective. For

example, practice saying "I'm having the thought that..." before a bad thought to build separation.

14. Flexibility Journaling: Keep a journal focusing on flexibility. Record instances where you successfully adapted to change or examined alternate perspectives. Reflect on these experiences to reinforce flexible thinking patterns.

15. Sensory Flexibility: Practice enduring and adapting to varied sensory experiences in a regulated manner. This can involve gradually introducing oneself to different textures, noises, or visual stimuli that you generally find problematic.

Enhancing flexibility in thoughts and emotional responses is a lengthy process that requires regular effort and patience. It's vital to approach this process with self-compassion, realizing that change can be tough, especially for those with autism who may find comfort in habit and predictability.

By frequently participating in these exercises and tactics, adults with autism can gradually expand their cognitive and emotional repertoire, leading to more adaptive responses to the complexities and unpredictabilities of daily life. This greater flexibility not only benefits mood control but can also contribute to improved problem-solving skills, social relationships, and overall quality of life.

Logical Analysis as an Emotional Regulation Tool

For many adults with autism, logical analysis can be a helpful tool for emotional management. This technique exploits the often-strong analytical talents and penchant for systematic thinking that many autistic individuals possess. By applying logical reasoning to emotional events, it's possible to acquire clarity, lower emotional intensity, and develop more efficient coping techniques. **Here's**

how to utilize logical analysis as an emotional management tool:

1. Emotion Categorization: Create a systematic categorization of emotions. This might include constructing a full taxonomy of emotional states, complete with descriptions, physical sensations, and typical triggers. Having a clear, rational structure for understanding emotions might make them feel more controllable.

2. Emotional Cause-and-Effect Analysis: Develop flowcharts or decision trees that map out the relationships between events, thoughts, and emotional responses. This graphic representation can aid in finding trends and intervention spots in emotional processes.

3. Probability Assessment: When dealing with anxiety or worry, utilize probability calculations to determine the possibility of feared consequences. Assign numerical probabilities to numerous

scenarios and compute the total probability of a negative outcome. This can help in putting issues into perspective.

4. Cost-Benefit Analysis: Apply a rigorous cost-benefit analysis to emotional emotions and prospective responses. Create a table detailing the advantages and downsides of alternative emotional responses or coping mechanisms, providing numerical values to each component if helpful.

5. Emotion Intensity Scaling: Develop an accurate, numerically-based scale for emotion intensity. Instead of ambiguous phrases like "very angry," use a 1-100 scale with clearly defined benchmarks. This enables more accurate tracking and analysis of emotional states throughout time.

6. rational Questioning: Develop a series of rational questions to ask oneself when experiencing powerful emotions. These can include: "What evidence supports this emotional response?" "Is

this emotion proportional to the situation?" "What are the logical consequences of acting on this emotion?"

7. Emotional Data Collection: Treat your emotional experiences as data pieces. Keep a careful diary of emotional episodes, including triggers, severity, length, and results. Analyze this data to uncover trends and patterns, which can inform more logical approaches to emotional regulation.

8. Cognitive Distortion Identification: Learn about common cognitive distortions (e.g., all-or-nothing thinking, overgeneralization) and establish a systematic strategy for spotting these in your thought processes. Create a checklist or flowchart to help in spotting and combating these logical fallacies.

9. Scenario Planning: Use logical analysis to construct extensive scenario plans for addressing tough emotional circumstances. Create decision

trees that lay out potential emotional triggers and planned responses, considering numerous possible outcomes.

10. Emotional Algorithm Development: Create personal algorithms or flow charts for navigating emotional situations. These can serve as step-by-step guidance for processing and responding to emotions in a logical, disciplined manner.

11. Fact vs. Interpretation Separation: Practice separating objective facts from subjective interpretations. When assessing an emotional scenario, make two unique lists: one for verified facts and another for interpretations or assumptions. This can aid in detecting when emotional responses might be based on misinterpretations.

12. Logical Reframing: Develop a way for logically reframing emotional thoughts. This can involve

constructing a pattern for translating emotive comments into more reasonable, balanced ones. For example, "I'm a complete failure" could be reframed as "I have experienced a setback in one area of my life."

13. Emotional Hypothesis Testing: Treat emotional beliefs as hypotheses to be tested. Develop experiments to challenge or verify emotional preconceptions. For instance, if you feel you'll be overwhelmed in a social environment, develop a systematic experiment to evaluate this idea, complete with clear criteria for success or failure.

14. Systematic Relaxation Logic: Apply logical thinking to relaxation practices. Break down relaxing processes into simple, logical steps. Create a flowchart for progressive muscle relaxation or deep breathing exercises, concentrating on the logical progression of physical states.

15. Emotion-Action Consequence Mapping: Develop thorough maps of the potential effects of emotionally-driven acts. This can aid in making more logical decisions about how to respond to emotional urges.

16. Logical Emotional Vocabulary: Create a precise, logically-defined emotional vocabulary. This might involve setting precise, objective definitions for emotional terminology, and decreasing ambiguity in how you explain and think about emotions.

17. Problem-Solving Frameworks: Adapt formal problem-solving frameworks (like the scientific method or engineering design process) to emotional challenges. Apply these organized ways to assessing and managing emotional concerns.

By applying these logical analytical approaches, adults with autism can approach emotional regulation in a way that feels more natural and aligned with their cognitive abilities. This method can provide a sense of control and insight in the sometimes chaotic world of emotions.

It's crucial to realize that while logical analysis can be a great tool, emotions aren't necessarily logical. The goal isn't to eradicate emotions or to always react logically, but rather to employ logical analysis as one tool among many for understanding and managing emotional events. Combining this method with other emotion regulation strategies can lead to a more comprehensive and successful emotional management system.

Chapter Five

Physiological Strategies for Emotional Balance

The Body-Emotion Connection in Autism

The relationship between the body and emotions is broad and diverse, and this connection takes on particular aspects in individuals with autism. Understanding this body-emotion connection is vital for establishing successful physiological solutions for emotional equilibrium.

In autism, sensory processing abnormalities play a key role in the body-emotion link. Many autistic individuals exhibit heightened sensory sensitivity or atypical sensory processing, which can directly influence emotional states. For example, some textures could evoke extreme feelings of discomfort or fear, whereas specific sounds or visual stimuli might generate serenity or delight. This sensory-emotional relationship is generally stronger in autism than in neurotypical individuals, making it an important factor in emotional management measures.

Interoception, the awareness of the internal condition of the body, is another crucial part of the body-emotion relationship in autism. Some autistic individuals report issues with interoception, which can impede the process of perceiving and responding to emotional experiences. For instance, an autistic individual could not readily identify physical sensations linked with worry (such as higher heart rate or muscle tension) as being related to an emotional state. Improving interoceptive awareness can be a beneficial approach to enhancing emotional regulation.

The autonomic nerve system, which governs numerous physical functions, typically acts differently in autistic individuals. Some study suggests that autistic people may have a more reactive sympathetic nervous system (responsible for the "fight or flight" reaction) and may have problems controlling the parasympathetic nervous system (responsible for "rest and digest" activities). This can lead to more powerful or protracted physiological responses to emotional stimuli, making emotion control more complex.

Stress responses in autism can also be atypical. Autistic individuals could have a lower threshold for stress, indicating that seemingly slight stressors can cause major physiological and emotional responses. Additionally, the recovery time from stressful situations may be longer, leading to prolonged episodes of emotional dysregulation.

The body-emotion connection in autism also emerges in stimming behaviors (self-stimulatory activities like hand-flapping, rocking, or repeated movements). These activities typically function as a way of emotional regulation, helping to relax the nervous system or convey overwhelming feelings. Understanding the regulation function of stimming is vital for building comprehensive emotional balance techniques.

Sleep patterns and circadian rhythms, which are intimately tied to emotional regulation, can be altered in autism. Many autistic individuals encounter sleep issues, which can increase emotional concerns and damage general well-being. Addressing sleep difficulties can be a crucial component of physiological methods for emotional equilibrium.

Gastrointestinal (GI) disorders are more common in autistic individuals and can severely impair emotional states. The gut-brain axis, which refers to the bidirectional communication between the gastrointestinal tract and the central nervous system, has a function in mood regulation. GI discomfort or dysfunction might contribute to irritation, anxiety, or other emotional difficulties.

Motor abnormalities in autism, such as issues with motor planning or coordination, can significantly influence emotional states. Physical discomfort or frustration originating from motor limitations might impair mood and emotional regulation.

Hormonal influences on emotions may also present differently in autism. Some study suggests that autistic individuals can have abnormal responses to oxytocin, a hormone important in social bonding and emotional regulation. Understanding these hormonal variances might inform more tailored methods for emotional balance.

The body-emotion connection in autism also extends to alexithymia, a disease defined by difficulties detecting and describing emotions, which is more prevalent in autistic individuals.

Alexithymia can complicate the process of integrating bodily sensations with emotional experiences, making it vital to develop solutions that bridge this gap.

Recognizing and utilizing the specific characteristics of the body-emotion connection in autism is vital for establishing successful physiological techniques for emotional balance. **This might involve:**

1. Developing individualized sensory profiles to understand how varied sensory inputs impact emotional states.
2. Practicing interoceptive awareness activities helps improve the recognition of internal physical states and their connection to emotions.
3. Implementing tactics to support autonomic nervous system modulation, such as deep pressure techniques or particular breathing exercises.
4. Acknowledging and promoting healthy stimming habits as a technique of emotional control.

5. Addressing sleep hygiene and maintaining consistent sleep routines to improve general emotional equilibrium.

6. Considering dietary considerations and gut health as part of a comprehensive approach to emotional control.

7. Incorporating movement and physical activities that assist both motor skills and emotional regulation.

By recognizing and working with the particular components of the body-emotion link in autism, individuals can develop more effective and tailored techniques for reaching emotional balance. This physiological approach, along with cognitive and behavioral methods, can give a comprehensive toolkit for emotional control in autism.

Autism-Friendly Breathing and Relaxation Techniques

Breathing and relaxation techniques can be important tools for emotional regulation, but they often need to be tailored to suit the special needs and preferences of autistic individuals. **Here are some autism-friendly ways to breathe and relaxation:**

1. Visual Breathing Guides: Many autistic individuals are visual learners. Create or use graphic guides for breathing exercises. This could be in the form of dynamic images that expand and contract, replicating the rhythm of breath, or simple diagrams that depict the breathing process. Apps or websites that offer visual breathing cues might be extremely helpful.

2. Structured Breathing Patterns: Develop clear, structured breathing patterns with defined counts

for inhaling, holding, and expelling. For example, the 4-7-8 technique (inhale for 4 counts, hold for 7, exhale for 8) provides a clear structure that may be readily followed and repeated.

3. Sensory-Enhanced Breathing: Incorporate sensory aspects into breathing exercises to make them more engaging and effective. This might involve:
- Using a favorite perfume during deep breathing exercises
- Holding a textured object that's pinched on inhale and released on exhale
- Using a swing or rocking chair to produce a rhythmic movement coordinated with breathing

4. Progressive Muscle Relaxation (PMR) with explicit Instructions: Adapt PMR techniques to incorporate very explicit, precise instructions. Create a script that carefully walks through tensing and relaxing each muscle group, using specific wording and avoiding misleading phrases.

5. Weighted Relaxation: Utilize weighted blankets or lap pads during relaxation activities. The deep pressure can assist soothe the nervous system and boost the relaxation response.

6. unique Interest Integration: Incorporate components of unique interests into relaxing techniques. For example, if an individual is interested in space, coach them through a "space breathing" exercise where they envision breathing in stardust and exhaling space debris.

7. Technology-Aided Relaxation: Use apps or devices developed for relaxation that correspond with autistic inclinations. This can include biofeedback devices that provide visual or tactile input on physiological states, helping to make the relaxing process more real and measurable.

8. Rhythm-Based Breathing: Use music or rhythmic sounds to guide breathing. Create playlists with

music that has a tempo ideal for quiet breathing, or utilize metronome apps to set a steady breathing cadence.

9. Body Scan with Sensory Focus: Adapt body scan meditations to include a focus on distinct sensory experiences throughout the body. This can help in establishing bodily awareness and can be very grounding for autistic individuals.

10. Yoga for Autism: Adapt yoga techniques to suit autistic inclinations. This can involve presenting clear, literal directions for positions, providing visual guidance, and focusing on stances that offer proprioceptive input.

11. attentive strimming: Incorporate attentive awareness into favorite stimming behaviors. Guide individuals to focus their attention on the sensory sensation of their stim, using it as an anchor for mindfulness practice.

12. Breath Counting: Offer easy breath-counting activities. This combines the benefits of breathwork with the regimented pattern of counting, which many autistic individuals find comforting.

13. Nature-Based Relaxation: For those who find comfort in nature, construct relaxation routines that involve natural aspects. This could involve imagining natural scenery, listening to nature sounds, or practicing relaxing techniques outdoors.

14. Social Story Relaxation: Develop social stories that guide through relaxation processes. These stories can lend a narrative structure to relaxation, making it more accessible and understanding.

15. Pressure Point Relaxation: Teach simple acupressure techniques that can be self-administered. This gives a tactile component to relaxing and might be helpful for persons who want physical sensory input.

16. Repetitive Phrase Meditation: Use basic, repetitive words or mantras as a focus for meditation. This can provide an organized approach to mindfulness that corresponds well with the preference for repetition that many autistic individuals exhibit.

17. Tense-and-Release Exercises: Develop easy tense-and-release exercises that may be done quietly in diverse circumstances. This gives a simple approach to reducing physical tension and controlling emotions.

When introducing these strategies, it's vital to:

- Provide explicit, step-by-step directions
- Allow for progressive introduction and practice
- Be open to alterations based on individual preferences and sensory needs
- Encourage frequent practice to increase familiarity and effectiveness

- Recognize that what works for one autistic individual may not work for another

By adjusting breathing and relaxation techniques to fit autistic tastes and requirements, these strong tools for emotional regulation become more accessible and effective. The objective is to find techniques that resonate with the individual, harmonizing with their sensory preferences, cognitive style, and personal interests. With practice, these autism-friendly breathing and relaxation techniques can become useful resources for maintaining emotional balance and managing stress.

Physical Activity and Its Role in Emotion Regulation

Physical activity has a critical role in emotion regulation for adults with autism, offering a potent tool for controlling stress, anxiety, and mood changes. The benefits of physical activity extend beyond general health and fitness, directly benefiting emotional well-being through multiple physiological and psychological systems. **Here's an in-depth look at how physical activity can be efficiently utilized for emotion control in autism:**

1. Neurotransmitter Regulation: Physical exercise stimulates the production of neurotransmitters like serotonin, dopamine, and norepinephrine. These molecules play a critical role in mood regulation and can help ease feelings of anxiety and sadness, which are typical co-occurring illnesses in autism.

2. Stress Reduction: Exercise helps reduce levels of stress hormones like cortisol while increasing the creation of endorphins, the body's natural mood lifters. This can be particularly advantageous for autistic individuals who may suffer heightened stress responses.

3. Sensory Regulation: Many forms of physical activity produce proprioceptive and vestibular input, which can be relaxing and organizing for the nervous system. Activities like jumping, swinging, or hard lifting can aid with sensory control, perhaps lowering emotional distress.

4. Routine and Structure: Incorporating regular physical activity into daily routines can create a sense of structure and predictability, which many autistic individuals find comfortable. This systematic approach to exercise can itself become a tool for emotional management.

5. Improved Sleep: Regular physical activity can help regulate sleep patterns, which are often interrupted with autism. Better sleep quality can lead to enhanced emotional regulation during waking hours.

6. Increased Body Awareness: Engaging in physical activities can enhance interoceptive awareness, helping autistic individuals become more attuned to their physiological states and, as a consequence, their emotional ones.

7. Social Connection: Group activities or team sports, when conducted in a supportive and inclusive manner, can create opportunities for social contact and connection, thereby boosting emotional well-being.

8. Outlet for Emotional Communication: Physical activities can serve as a healthy outlet for expressing and processing emotions, especially for persons who may struggle with verbal communication of sentiments.

9. Cognitive Benefits: Regular exercise has been demonstrated to improve executive functioning skills, which are commonly challenged with autism.

Better executive function can contribute to greater emotional management abilities.

10. Self-Esteem enhancement: Achieving fitness objectives or increasing physical skills can enhance self-esteem and confidence, favorably boosting overall emotional well-being.

When using physical activity as an emotion management strategy for autistic adults, consider the following strategies:

- Personalized Approach: Tailor physical exercises to individual interests, sensory preferences, and motor abilities. What works for one individual may not work for another.

- Structured Exercise Programs: Develop explicit, step-by-step exercise regimens. Visual schedules or video tutorials can help establish organization and consistency.

- Sensory-Friendly situations: Choose or develop workout situations that are sensory-friendly. This might require altering lighting, sound levels, or the number of people present.

- Incorporate particular Interests: Where possible, integrate particular interests into physical activity. For example, if someone is interested in animals, activities could include yoga positions named after animals or nature hikes focusing on wildlife observation.

- Gradual Introduction: Introduce new physical activities gradually to minimize overwhelm. Start with small durations and slowly increase time and intensity.

- Consistency: Encourage regular, consistent engagement in physical activities rather than periodic intense sessions.

- Mindful Movement: Incorporate mindfulness into physical activities, fostering awareness of physiological sensations and motions. This can boost the emotional management benefits.

- Use of Technology: Utilize fitness trackers or apps that provide visual representations of progress, which can be motivational and help in understanding the body's responses to exercise.

- Adaptive Equipment: Consider employing adaptive equipment or adaptations to make activities more accessible and pleasurable.

- Combination with Other Strategies: Pair physical activities with other mood management approaches, such as deep breathing or positive self-talk.

- Post-Activity introspection: Encourage introspection after physical activity to help identify the emotional repercussions. This can raise awareness of the body-emotion relationship.

- Social Support: If appropriate, enlist family members, friends, or support workers in physical activities to provide encouragement and social connection.

Examples of autism-friendly physical activity for emotion regulation:

1. Swimming or water therapy: Provides full-body sensory input and can be soothing.
2. Martial arts: Offers structure, and routine, and helps increase body awareness and self-control.
3. Yoga or tai chi: Combines physical movement with breathing and mindfulness activities.
4. Trampolining: Provides vestibular and proprioceptive input, which can be regulated.
5. Cycling: Offers repeated action and can be done solo or socially.

6. Weight training: Provides deep pressure input and may be readily planned and progressed.

7. Dance: Can be adaptive to many ability levels and gives an expressive release.

8. Rock climbing: Offers problem-solving elements combined with physical exertion.

9. Walking or trekking in nature: Combines exercise with the relaxing effects of nature.

By strategically incorporating physical activity into daily life, autistic persons can harness its strong impact on emotional regulation. The idea is to discover activities that are pleasurable, sustainable, and consistent with individual needs and preferences. When done consistently, physical activity can become a cornerstone of good emotion management, contributing to overall well-being and quality of life for persons with autism.

Chapter Six

Mindfulness and Grounding Practices for Autism

Adapting Mindfulness for the Autistic Experience

Mindfulness, the practice of focusing one's attention on the present moment without judgment, can be a valuable tool for emotional regulation and overall well-being. However, standard mindfulness activities may need to be altered to meet the particular cognitive and sensory profiles of autistic individuals. **Here's how mindfulness can be adjusted for the autistic experience:**

1. Concrete directions: Provide clear, detailed directions for mindfulness activities. Instead of broad commands like "focus on your breath," offer explicit guidance such as "notice the air entering your nostrils, filling your lungs, and then leaving your body." Use literal language and avoid metaphors that can be confusing.

2. Visual Supports: Incorporate visual aids to support mindfulness practice. This could contain diagrams of the body for body scan exercises, visual timers to show the duration of practice, or visuals depicting different feelings or emotions to focus on during mindfulness activities.

3. Structured Approach: Develop a structured, step-by-step approach to mindfulness sessions. Create a visual timetable or checklist of the many components of the practice, providing for a predictable and ordered experience.

4. Sensory-Friendly surroundings: Customize the surroundings to minimize sensory disturbances. This can mean reducing lighting, utilizing noise-canceling headphones, or practicing in a room with little visual distraction. Allow the use of comfort objects or fidget toys if they aid with focus.

5. Short Duration: Start with small mindfulness sessions, possibly just a few minutes long, then gradually expand the duration as tolerance and interest build. It's better to have consistent short practices than rare lengthy ones.

6. Focus on Physical Sensations: For autistic individuals who may struggle with abstract concepts, focus mindfulness activities on real, physical sensations. This could be noticing the weight of the body on a chair, the feel of garments against the skin, or the temperature of the air.

7. Incorporate Movement: For people who find it tough to sit motionless, integrate movement into

mindfulness activities. This could include strolling meditation, moderate stretching, or even mindful stimming (repetitive movements typically utilized by autistic individuals for self-regulation).

8. Use of Technology: Utilize applications or other tools created for mindfulness that correspond with autistic tastes. Look for applications that give visual instruction, customizable settings, and progress tracking.

9. unique Interest Integration: Incorporate elements of unique interests into mindfulness practice. For example, if someone is interested in space, coach them through a mindfulness practice thinking they are drifting calmly among the stars.

10. Emotion-Free Start: Begin with mindfulness exercises that don't require emotional awareness, concentrating instead on bodily sensations or external objects. As comfort with the practice

grows, gradually include exercises involving emotional awareness.

11. Customized Metaphors: If employing metaphors in guided mindfulness, ensure they resonate with the autistic experience. For instance, instead of visualizing ideas as clouds passing by (which can be too abstract), employ a metaphor of sorting objects or arranging a collection.

12. Mindful Stimming: Develop mindfulness exercises around favored stimming habits. Guide individuals to focus their whole attention on the sensory sensation of their stim, using it as an anchor for present-moment awareness.

13. Social Story Approach: Create social stories that explain the notion of mindfulness and guide through different activities. This story method can make mindfulness more accessible and understanding.

14. Non-Verbal Options: Offer mindfulness practices that don't demand verbal responses or interactions. This can be particularly useful for non-speaking autistic individuals or those who experience selective mutism.

15. Sensory Mindfulness Kit: Develop a personalized kit containing items that engage multiple senses (e.g., fragrant oils, textured objects, graphic cards) to be utilized during mindfulness practice.

16. Mindful Listening: For persons who are auditory processors, focus on mindful listening techniques. This could be paying attention to environmental sounds or listening to music thoughtfully.

17. Flexibility in Practice: Allow for flexibility in how mindfulness is practiced. Some may prefer lying down instead of sitting or may need to take pauses. The purpose is to make the practice

accessible and beneficial, not to stick exactly to traditional procedures.

By adjusting mindfulness practices in these ways, autistic individuals can access the benefits of mindfulness in a way that feels comfortable and meaningful to them. It's crucial to remember that what works for one person may not work for another, therefore promoting experimentation and personalization in building a mindfulness practice.

Consistency is crucial in obtaining the advantages of mindfulness. Encourage frequent practice, even if it's just for a few minutes a day. Over time, mindfulness can become a significant technique for emotional regulation, stress reduction, and overall well-being for autistic individuals.

Sensory Grounding Exercises

Sensory grounding exercises are particularly good for autistic individuals since they can assist regulate sensory overload, reduce anxiety, and increase emotional regulation. These exercises include employing sensory input to anchor oneself in the present moment, providing a sense of stability and tranquility. **Here's a full look at sensory grounding techniques geared toward autism:**

1. The 5-4-3-2-1 Technique: This traditional grounding practice can be altered for autistic individuals by focusing on preferred or neutral sensory stimuli. Guide the person to identify:
- 5 things they can see
- 4 things they can touch
- 3 things they can hear

- 2 items they can smell
- 1 item they can taste

Provide a visual checklist or use objects to symbolize each sensation, making the task more real.

2. Texture Exploration: Create a box of varied textured items (e.g., smooth stones, abrasive sandpaper, soft fabric, squishy stress balls). Encourage careful exploration of these textures, focusing on the feelings in the fingertips.

3. Weighted Grounding: Use weighted things like blankets, vests, or lap pads. The deep pressure input can be immensely relaxing and centering for many autistic persons.

4. Temperature Contrast: Provide safe ways to experience temperature contrasts, such as holding a chilled water bottle or utilizing a microwaveable heat pack. The distinct temperature sensation can

assist in redirecting concentration and provide grounding.

5. Olfactory Grounding: Use favored scents in the form of essential oils, scented putty, or scratch-and-sniff stickers. Encourage thorough breathing of these scents as a grounding strategy.

6. Visual Grounding with particular Interests: Create a grounding box loaded with visually appealing items connected to particular interests. This could include images, small items, or written facts. Engaging with these items can bring both grounding and comfort.

7. Auditory Grounding: Develop a playlist of peaceful sounds or music. This could include nature noises, white noise, or favorite songs. Use noise-canceling headphones to enhance the experience if background noise is distressing.

8. Proprioceptive Input: Engage in activities that produce strong proprioceptive input, such as wall push-ups, squeezing stress balls, or utilizing resistance bands. These practices might aid with body awareness and grounding.

9. Mindful Eating: Use small, highly flavored items (e.g., mints, sour candies) for taste-based grounding. Guide the individual to focus totally on the taste and texture of the food.

10. Grounding Jar: Create a visual grounding tool by filling a clear jar with water and glitter or small objects. Shaking the jar and watching the contents settle may be both visually grounded and calming.

11. Vestibular Grounding: For people who seek vestibular input, regulated rocking in a rocking chair or gently swinging might be grounding. Always ensure the movement is slow and rhythmic.

12. Breath-Focused Grounding: Use visual aids like pinwheels or bubbles to make breath-focused grounding more concrete and engaging.

13. Nature Grounding: If feasible, incorporate natural components into grounding activities. This could involve gripping smooth rocks, feeling grass underfoot, or listening to running water.

14. Calming Pressure Points: Teach easy acupressure techniques that can be self-administered, such as gently pressing on the fleshy area between the eyebrows or between the thumb and index finger.

15. Repetitive Movement: Engage in repetitive, rhythmic motions that the individual finds comforting, such as swaying, finger tapping, or gentle rocking. Guide them to focus their attention totally on the sensation of the movement.

16. Color Grounding: Use color as a focus for grounding. This could involve looking for objects of a given color in the area or employing color-changing lights as a visual focus.

17. Tactile Fidgets: Provide a range of tactile fidget items (e.g., putty, textured tangles, worry stones) that can be manipulated for sensory input and grounding.

18. Body Outline: Use a body outline sketch and help the participant color in places where they experience tension or intense sensations, creating body awareness and grounding.

19. Sensory Bottles: Create personalized sensory bottles filled with water and various little things. Shaking and viewing these bottles can be both visually grounded and calming.

20. Grounding practice: Develop a personalized grounding practice that integrates preferred

sensory inputs. This could be a series of events (e.g., deep pressure, then scent, sound) that can be followed in times of stress.

When applying these sensory grounding techniques, consider the following:

- Personalization: What works for one autistic individual may not work for another. Experiment with different ways to see what's most effective.
- Accessibility: Ensure that grounding instruments or procedures are easily accessible, especially in potentially stressful situations.
- Practice: Encourage regular practice of grounding techniques when calm, so they're easier to execute during times of stress.
- Sensory Preferences: Be cognizant of individual sensory preferences and aversions. Avoid employing sensory cues that could be overwhelming or disturbing.

- Gradual Introduction: Introduce new grounding techniques progressively and one at a time to prevent overload.
- Safety: Ensure all grounding exercises and instruments are safe, especially for persons who might have difficulties regulating their use.

By combining a range of sensory grounding exercises into daily life, autistic individuals can acquire a potent arsenal for regulating sensory overload, lowering anxiety, and increasing overall emotional regulation. These approaches can provide a sense of control and stability, helping patients navigate the often overwhelming sensory world with greater ease and confidence.

Incorporating Special Interests into Mindfulness Practice

Incorporating particular interests into mindfulness practice can be a highly effective strategy to engage autistic individuals in mindfulness and make it more meaningful and pleasurable for them. Special interests, frequently characterized by intense focus and extensive knowledge, can serve as effective anchors for attention and motivation in mindfulness practice. **Here's how to effectively integrate special hobbies into mindfulness:**

1. Interest-Themed Guided Meditations: Create unique guided meditations based on the individual's special interests. For example, if someone is interested in space, construct a meditation that brings them through a tranquil voyage across the cosmos, combining accurate facts about planets and stars.

2. Mindful Engagement with Interest-connected Objects: Use objects connected to the unique interest as focuses for mindfulness practice. For instance, if trains are a specific interest, practice

careful observation of a model train, noticing its intricacies, colors, and textures.

3. Specific Interest Visualizations: Develop visualization exercises that combine elements of the specific interest. For a person interested in history, this can mean envisioning oneself calmly viewing historical events or exploring ancient landscapes.

4. Fact-Based Mindfulness: For interests that include gathering facts or data, design mindfulness activities that involve deliberately and mindfully reciting or mentally examining these facts. This can act as a sort of mantra meditation.

5. Interest-Inspired Body Scans: Adapt typical body scan meditations to accommodate the unique interest. For example, for someone interested in botany, walk them through a body scan where they picture roots emerging from their feet, leaves sprouting from their arms, etc.

6. Mindful Research: Guide the individual in practicing mindfulness while engaging in research concerning their unique interest. This could involve attentively reading a relevant book or article, paying close attention to each word, and absorbing the material with full consciousness.

7. Creative Mindfulness: For pursuits that entail creativity (like art or music), include mindfulness in the creative process. This can be mindfully drawing, painting, or composing, with complete attention to each movement or sound.

8. Mindful Collections: If collecting items related to a unique interest is part of the passion, practice mindful observation and organizing of these collections. Guide the individual to completely engage their senses in analyzing and arranging their acquired items.

9. Passion-based Mindful Movement: Create movement-based mindfulness practices inspired by

the unique passion. For instance, if animals are of interest, construct a series of mindful movements based on animal behaviors or yoga positions named after animals.

10. Sensory examination of Interest Items: Guide a sensory-focused examination of items connected to the special interest. This could involve actively touching, smelling, and visually analyzing objects, completely engaging with their sensory characteristics.

11. Mindful Listening to Interest-Related noises: If the special interest includes associated noises (e.g., bird calls for an interest in ornithology), practice mindful listening activities focused on these sounds.

12. particular Interest Gratitude Practice: Develop a gratitude meditation centered on components of the particular interest, guiding the individual to

mindfully contemplate and appreciate different elements of their passion.

13. Mindful Photography: For visual interests, incorporate mindfulness into photography. Guide the participant in actively studying their environment to collect photos linked to their interest, focusing fully on the visual details.

14. Interest-Based Loving-Kindness Meditation: Adapt loving-kindness meditation to incorporate elements of the unique interest. For example, for someone interested in ecosystems, help them by sending pleasant wishes to different areas of an ecosystem.

15. Mindful writing: Encourages mindful writing about the specific interest, guiding the individual to write with full awareness, noting thoughts and feelings that come as they interact with their passion.

16. Virtual Reality Mindfulness: If appropriate, use VR technology to create immersive mindfulness experiences connected to the unique interest, such as a virtual museum tour for an art fan.

17. Mindful Skill Practice: If the unique interest involves improving specific skills, add mindfulness into skill practice sessions, concentrating full attention on each facet of the activity.

18. Interest-Themed Mindful Eating: For interests related to food or cooking, construct mindful eating exercises that focus on foods relevant to the interest, paying close attention to flavors, textures, and scents.

19. Mindful Watching: If the unique interest involves watching specific types of films or shows, guide the client in watching consciously, paying close attention to details and their reactions.

20. Mindful Social Engagement: For interests that include community engagement, practice mindfulness throughout interactions with people who share the interest, focusing on the present moment features of these social encounters.

When bringing special interests into mindfulness practice, consider the following:

- Personalization: Tailor the mindfulness practices to the exact components of the interest that the individual finds most engaging.
- Flexibility: Be open to altering practices based on how the individual responds. What works one day might not work the next.
- Balance: While using unique interests might make mindfulness more accessible, also carefully teach more general mindfulness practices over time.
- Respect: Treat the specific interest with respect and real interest, as it's often a vitally essential part of the autistic individual's identity.

- Growth: Use the unique interest as a beginning point, but also as a bridge to explore other areas of mindfulness practice.
- Sensory Considerations: Be attentive to any sensory sensitivities related to the special interest and alter practices accordingly.
- Ethical Considerations: Ensure that the mindfulness practices associated with the unique interest are ethical and do not encourage any potentially damaging features of intense interests.

By mindfully adding specific interests into mindfulness practice, autistic individuals might create a more personal and meaningful connection to mindfulness. This technique not only makes mindfulness more accessible and pleasurable but also harnesses the inherent attention and engagement associated with unique interests to enhance the practice. Over time, this can lead to increased emotional control, less stress, and enhanced general well-being, all while acknowledging and supporting the unique passions of autistic individuals.

Chapter Seven

Communication and Social-Emotional Strategies

Expressing Emotions Effectively in Various Social Contexts

For adults with autism, expressing emotions properly in diverse social circumstances can be a challenging issue. The intricacies of social communication, combined with the distinctive emotional experiences associated with autism, often present hurdles to clear emotional expression. However, with experience and specific techniques, individuals can learn more effective ways to communicate their feelings across diverse social circumstances.

One crucial part of effective emotional expression is recognizing the context-dependent nature of communication. What may be appropriate in a casual situation with friends might not be suitable in a professional environment. Adults with autism can benefit from constructing a mental framework or checklist to examine the social situation before expressing feelings. This framework could incorporate variables such as the relationship with the persons there, the formality of the environment, and the cultural norms at play.

Developing a strong emotional vocabulary is vital for precise communication. Many adults with autism find it beneficial to construct a personalized lexicon of emotional phrases, replete with definitions and examples. This can aid in effectively understanding and expressing subtle emotions, expanding beyond basic categories like "happy" or "sad" to more specific descriptions like "contentment," "frustration," or "anticipation."

Non-verbal communication plays a crucial role in emotional expression, and this can be an area of difficulty for certain individuals with autism. Practicing facial expressions, tone of voice, and body language in front of a mirror or with a trusted friend can assist develop these skills. Additionally, learning to notice and interpret others' non-verbal signs helps strengthen overall emotional communication.

For instances where instant verbal representation is problematic, alternate communication methods can be essential. This can include using written notes, text messages, or even pre-prepared scripts for frequent emotional events. Some individuals find visual tools, such as emotion wheels or color-coded cards, helpful in articulating their sentiments quickly and precisely.

It's crucial to acknowledge that direct and honest communication, frequently a strength for those with autism, may be incredibly beneficial in emotional expression. However, learning to combine this directness with social subtlety is crucial. Practicing phrases that soften communication without compromising honesty might be helpful, such as "I feel..." statements or prefacing uncomfortable emotions with acknowledgments of the other person's perspective.

Lastly, self-advocacy plays a significant part in effective emotional expression. Adults with autism should feel confident to convey their communication style and needs to others when appropriate. This can involve teaching colleagues, acquaintances, or partners about autism and how it affects emotional expression, so providing a more understanding and supportive atmosphere for communication.

Navigating Social Situations and Emotional Challenges

Navigating social situations and overcoming the related emotional hurdles is an important ability for adults with autism. Social interactions typically entail unwritten norms, subtle clues, and unforeseen variables that might be overpowering or perplexing. However, with the correct tactics and mindset, these issues can be efficiently controlled.

One essential technique is to prepare for social interactions in advance. This could involve researching the event or environment, contemplating probable subjects of conversation, and mentally practicing standard social scripts. Creating a "social toolkit" with conversation starters, escape options, and coping skills can create a sense of security and readiness.

Understanding and regulating sensory sensitivities is vital in navigating social situations. Identifying potential sensory triggers in diverse contexts and having ways to manage them can prevent emotional overwhelm. This can involve wearing noise-canceling headphones, choosing to sit near exits, or taking regular breaks in quieter places.

Developing a repertoire of coping skills for in-the-moment emotional issues is vital. These could include grounding strategies like deep breathing or tactile stimulation, using positive self-talk, or employing cognitive restructuring to reframe stressful events. Having a discrete signal or code phrase to indicate distress to a trusted companion might also be beneficial.

Practicing mindfulness and self-awareness can considerably boost social navigation skills. By tuning into one's emotional state and identifying early indicators of stress or overstimulation, individuals can make proactive efforts to manage their emotions before they become overwhelming. This could require stepping away for a short break, engaging in a relaxing activity, or altering one's level of social involvement.

Learning to set and communicate boundaries is another key component of managing social and emotional issues. This involves being able to decline invites when necessary, leaving events early if needed, and conveying personal needs properly. Practicing assertiveness in a way that balances self-care with social responsibility is a good skill to master.

For many adults with autism, adopting a systematic approach to social engagement can be beneficial. This could involve setting explicit goals for social interactions (e.g., talking to three new people or remaining for a defined amount of time), or employing social scripts for frequent circumstances. Over time, these frameworks can be gradually relaxed as familiarity and confidence build.

It's also crucial to discover and use personal strengths in social circumstances. Many individuals with autism have extensive knowledge or love for specialized areas, which can be wonderful conversation starters when presented responsibly. Learning to evaluate interest and engage in reciprocal discussion around these themes can turn a potential barrier into a social strength.

Lastly, fostering self-compassion is vital while facing social and emotional issues. Recognizing that everyone, neurotypical or neurodivergent, encounters social challenges might assist lessen self-criticism. Celebrating modest triumphs and viewing problems as chances for growth rather than failures can foster a more optimistic approach to social interactions.

Building and Utilizing a Support Network

For individuals with autism, developing and efficiently utilizing a support network is vital for emotional well-being and personal progress. A robust support network can give empathy, practical aid, and emotional reinforcement, helping persons navigate the difficulties of daily living and social interactions.

The first stage in developing a support network is identifying potential sources of support. This can include family members, friends, colleagues, mental health experts, support groups, and internet communities. It's crucial to examine a varied range of supports that can serve different needs – emotional, practical, social, and professional.

When creating relationships for support, clear communication about one's autism and specific requirements is crucial. This doesn't mean disclosing to everyone, but rather selectively sharing with persons who indicate understanding and readiness to support. Educating supporters about autism, personal obstacles, and strengths can help them provide more effective and individualized support.

Support groups designed for adults with autism can be useful. These organizations give a venue to exchange experiences, methods, and resources with those who fully understand the unique challenges of autism. They can also create a sense of community and belonging that may be difficult to discover elsewhere. Both in-person and online support groups can be effective, giving different advantages in terms of accessibility and comfort level.

Professional help is typically a critical component of a comprehensive support network. This can include psychologists, occupational therapists, or career counselors who specialize in dealing with adults with autism. These specialists can give tailored solutions for emotional control, social skills development, and life management.

Developing reciprocal relationships is vital in sustaining a healthy support network. While it's okay to receive support, finding ways to give back - whether via sharing knowledge, delivering practical aid, or simply being a good listener – may deepen relationships and create a sense of value and purpose.

Technology may play a crucial role in developing and maintaining a support network. Social networking platforms, autism-specific forums, and apps developed for social connection can help persons stay connected with supporters, discover new connections, and access resources and information.

It's vital to learn how to efficiently utilize the support network once it's built. This includes knowing when and how to ask for help, being precise about requirements, and respecting limits. Developing a personal "support plan" that defines different sources of support and when to use them can be helpful in times of stress or uncertainty.

Regular maintenance of the support network is crucial. This can involve organizing regular check-ins with important supporters, expressing gratitude for services received, and periodically reassessing the network to ensure it continues to suit evolving needs.

Lastly, it's crucial to remember that developing a support network is an ongoing effort. It may take time to locate the correct combination of supporters and to develop the skills to effectively utilize this network. Patience, tenacity, and self-compassion are crucial as this vital resource is developed and improved over time.

Chapter Eight

Managing Intense Emotional Experiences

Understanding Meltdowns and Shutdowns

Meltdowns and shutdowns are extreme emotional states typically associated with autism. While they can be tough and sometimes misunderstood, developing a deeper knowledge of these phenomena is vital for adults with autism and others who support them.

A meltdown can be described as an intense response to overwhelming events. It's generally characterized by a loss of behavioral control, which may be expressed as verbal outbursts, physical agitation, or aggressive behavior. Importantly, meltdowns are not planned or manipulative; rather, they're a response to acute stress, sensory overload, or emotional overwhelm. For adults with autism, meltdowns might feel like a complete lack of control over one's mental state and actions.

Shutdowns, on the other hand, represent the opposite extreme of the spectrum. During a shutdown, an individual may become non-responsive, withdrawn, and unable to communicate or process information properly. This state can be equated to a system overload, where the brain briefly "shuts off" to protect itself from more stress or stimulation.

Both meltdowns and shutdowns often arise from comparable triggers, including:

1. Sensory overload: Excessive loudness, light, or tactile stimulation
2. Changes in routine or unexpected events

3. Social pressures or misunderstandings
4. Difficulty in communication or self-expression
5. Accumulation of stress throughout time

It's vital to remember that these sensations are neurobiological responses, not behavioral choices. They often occur from a buildup of tension that may not be immediately evident to others or even to the individual experiencing them.

For individuals with autism, identifying the early indicators of an approaching meltdown or shutdown is crucial. These may include heightened anxiety, difficulties concentrating, bodily symptoms like headaches or muscle tightness, or a strong need to escape the current circumstance. Developing this self-awareness can be a helpful aid in handling unpleasant situations.

The impact of meltdowns and shutdowns can be severe, hurting personal relationships, work performance, and general quality of life. They can lead to feelings of embarrassment, frustration, and isolation, particularly if they occur in public or professional contexts. Therefore, it's necessary to face these situations with compassion and empathy, both for oneself and for others.

It's crucial to emphasize that while meltdowns and shutdowns are common with autism, they're not exclusive to it. Many neurotypical individuals may experience comparable symptoms under extreme stress. However, for adults with autism, these experiences may be more frequent, intense, or challenging to manage due to abnormalities in sensory processing, emotional regulation, and social comprehension.

By improving their awareness of meltdowns and shutdowns, adults with autism can begin to build more effective techniques for prevention, management, and recovery. This information also helps people to teach others, promoting greater understanding and support in their personal and professional lives.

Preventive Strategies and Early Intervention Techniques

Preventing meltdowns and shutdowns, or responding early when signals first arise, can dramatically enhance the quality of life for adults with autism. By applying proactive techniques and identifying early warning signals, individuals can frequently avoid or minimize the intensity of these stressful events.

One of the most effective preventive strategies is having a constant and predictable schedule. This creates a sense of security and decreases the risk of unforeseen shocks. However, as life is fundamentally unpredictable, it's also necessary to establish flexibility and coping skills for when routines are broken. This can involve preparing contingency plans for typical circumstances or exercising flexibility in low-stress conditions.

Sensory control is another key part of prevention. This involves:

1. Identifying personal sensory triggers and thresholds
2. Creating a sensory-friendly atmosphere at home and work
3. Using gear like noise-canceling headphones, sunglasses, or weighted blankets
4. Incorporating regular sensory breaks into daily routines

Stress management approaches play a significant part in prevention. Regular exercise, mindfulness practices, and engaging in unique interests can all help reduce overall stress levels, making persons more resilient to possible triggers. It's vital to make these activities a consistent part of one's routine, rather than merely resorting to them at times of severe stress.

Developing effective communication skills is vital for preventing misunderstandings that might lead to emotional escalation. **This might involve:**

1. Practicing straightforward communication
2. Learning to advocate for one's demands successfully
3. Using visual assistance or writing communication when verbal expression is problematic

Early intervention tactics are vital for handling situations when stress begins to build. The key is recognizing personal early warning indicators, which could include physical symptoms (e.g., elevated heart rate, muscle tension), cognitive changes (e.g., difficulty concentrating, racing thoughts), or emotional shifts (e.g., impatience, worry).

Once these indications are detected, early intervention measures might include:

1. Removing oneself from the uncomfortable environment if possible
2. Engaging in soothing activities (e.g., deep breathing, swimming, listening to music)
3. Using pre-prepared scripts or cards to communicate needs to others
4. Implementing grounding practices to stay present and centered

It's also important to construct a personal "emotional regulation toolkit" - a set of tactics and skills that can be rapidly accessed when stress begins to rise. This could include stuff like fidget toys, comfort objects, or printed reminders of coping skills.

For some adults with autism, medication recommended by a healthcare practitioner may play a role in treating anxiety or other disorders that contribute to meltdowns or shutdowns. If contemplating this option, it's crucial to work closely with a doctor who knows autism in adults.

Lastly, having a support network of understanding folks who can notice signals of distress and provide appropriate help is vital. This could include family members, friends, or colleagues who have been informed of the individual's requirements and preferred intervention tactics.

By concentrating on prevention and early intervention, adults with autism can greatly reduce the frequency and intensity of meltdowns and shutdowns, leading to increased emotional well-being and overall quality of life.

Recovery and Self-Care After Intense Emotional Episodes

Recovery and self-care following a meltdown or shutdown are key parts of emotional regulation for adults with autism. These intense experiences can be physically and emotionally taxing, and effective recovery is vital for restoring balance and preventing recurrent episodes.

Immediately after a meltdown or shutdown, it's crucial to prioritize safety and fundamental necessities. This could mean moving to a calm, safe area, managing any bodily discomfort, and ensuring hydration and nutrition. It's generally good to have a pre-prepared "recovery kit" immediately accessible, containing stuff like water, snacks, comfort objects, and any necessary sensory equipment.

Allow adequate time for healing. The period needed might vary substantially between persons and situations, ranging from hours to days. It's crucial to note that forcing oneself back into regular routines too quickly can lead to increased sensitivity to future episodes. If feasible, clear your schedule to allow for appropriate rest and processing time.

Engaging in relaxing activities can aid in emotional and sensory rehabilitation. These might include:

1. Engaging with unique interests or hobbies
2. Watching familiar, comforting movies or TV shows
3. Listening to relaxing music or nature sounds
4. Engaging in repetitive, relaxing activities (e.g., coloring, puzzles)
5. Spending time in nature, if that's personally calming

Physical self-care is equally vital. This might involve:

1. Getting proper sleep
2. Eating healthful meals
3. Gentle exercise or stretching
4. Taking a warm bath or shower
5. Using weighted blankets or pressure stimulation if found comforting

Cognitive processing of the incident can be useful, but timing is key. Some folks may demand rapid reflection, while others could require distance before analysis. **When ready, consider:**

1. Journaling on the experience
2. Discussing the event with a trustworthy friend or therapist
3. Analyzing triggers and effectiveness of coping methods utilized
4. Updating personal coping plans based on insights acquired

It's crucial to exercise self-compassion during the rehabilitation process. Meltdowns and shutdowns are not personal failures, but rather part of the autism experience. Avoid self-criticism and instead focus on self-understanding and growth.

Communication with individuals who may have been there or affected during the experience is necessary but should be approached when feeling adequately recovered. **This might involve:**

1. Explaining what transpired, if desired
2. Apologizing for any unintended injury, without self-blame
3. Discussing strategies for greater help in future scenarios

For some, re-establishing a routine can be a soothing part of healing. Gradually easing back into regular activities, starting with modest, predictable tasks, can help reestablish a sense of normalcy and control.

Lastly, regard the episode as a learning opportunity. Reflect on what led to the meltdown or shutdown, what techniques were useful, and what could be improved for future instances. This knowledge can be important in refining personal coping skills and preventative programs.

Remember, recovery is not a linear process. It's typical to experience residual effects or heightened sensitivity for some time following an intense emotional incident. Patience, self-compassion, and continuous self-care are crucial to effective rehabilitation and long-term emotional well-being for adults with autism.

Chapter Nine

Lifestyle Factors for Long-Term Emotional Well-being

Creating Autism-Friendly Routines and Structures

For adults with autism, adopting and sustaining autism-friendly routines and structures is critical for long-term emotional well-being. These routines create a sense of predictability and control, which can considerably reduce anxiety and tension in daily life.

The first step in building efficient routines is to understand personal needs and preferences. This comprises a detailed self-assessment of everyday activities, sensory sensitivities, energy levels, and stress triggers. Consider questions like: When are you most productive? What places help you feel calm? What hobbies sap your energy? This self-knowledge forms the foundation for establishing individualized routines.

When developing daily routines, it's crucial to achieve a balance between rigidity and flexibility. While predictability is reassuring, too rigid habits can lead to higher stress when unexpected changes occur. Build in buffer times between activities and have contingency plans for common disruptions. This technique helps retain the benefits of routine while fostering adaptability.

Visual aids can be highly helpful in keeping routines. These might include:

1. Detailed daily schedules
2. Task checklists
3. Color-coded calendars
4. Digital reminders or apps

Choose tools that match your unique preferences and cognitive type. Some folks might prefer paper planners, while others could find digital tools more effective.

Incorporate regular sensory breaks into your routine. These can assist minimize sensory overload and preserve emotional equilibrium throughout the day. **Sensory breaks might involve activities like:**

1. Short intervals of stimming
2. Listening to relaxing music
3. Engaging in deep-pressure activities
4. Spending time in a calm, darkly lit space

Creating transition rituals helps ease the change between different activities or surroundings. These might be simple things like taking three deep breaths before entering a new area or listening to specific music when moving from work to home.

Structure your environment to support your routines. **This might involve:**

1. Organizing your living place to minimize sensory pressures
2. Creating distinct areas for a specific activity
3. Using visual signals in your environment to support routine adherence

Don't forget to build in time for specific hobbies and fun activities. These can function as effective motivators and sources of comfort inside your routine.

Regularly assess and alter your procedures. What works well now might need adjusting when circumstances change. Set aside time frequently to review the success of your routines and make any adjustments.

Communicate your habits and needs to others around you. This may include family members, housemates, or colleagues. Clear communication can help others understand and support your requirements, eliminating potential disputes or misunderstandings.

Remember, the purpose of building autism-friendly routines and structures is to promote your well-being, not to create additional stress. Be patient with yourself while you establish and enhance these processes. With time and experience, well-designed routines can dramatically boost daily functioning and emotional stability for adults with autism.

The Role of Sleep, Nutrition, and Exercise in Emotional Stability

Sleep, nutrition, and exercise play key roles in sustaining emotional stability for adults with autism. These fundamental characteristics of physical health have a tremendous impact on mental and emotional well-being, often influencing sensory processing, stress management, and general mood regulation.

Sleep is particularly crucial for those with autism, who may be more prone to sleep disruptions. Poor sleep can worsen sensory sensitivity, increase irritation, and decrease cognitive function. **To increase sleep quality:**

1. Establish a constant sleep routine, especially on weekends
2. Create a relaxing nighttime routine to inform the body it's time to wind down
3. Optimize the sleep environment (e.g., pleasant temperature, low light, and noise)
4. Consider employing weighted blankets or white noise machines if helpful

5. Limit screen time and stimulating activities before bed
6. Be wary of caffeine and alcohol intake, especially in the evening

If sleep issues persist, speaking with a sleep specialist who understands autism can be beneficial.

Nutrition plays a vital impact in emotional stability. Some individuals with autism may have sensory sensitivities that affect their food, while others can have specific dietary demands. **General guidelines for dietary and mental well-being include:**

1. Maintaining steady blood sugar levels by eating regular, balanced meals
2. Including foods rich in omega-3 fatty acids, which enhance brain health
3. Ensuring appropriate consumption of vitamins and minerals, notably B vitamins and magnesium

4. Staying hydrated throughout the day

5. Being cognizant of individual allergies to certain meals

6. Considering the impact of caffeine and sugar on mood and energy levels

For some adults with autism, working with a dietitian to design a specific food plan can be useful in maintaining both physical health and mental stability.

Exercise is a great technique for emotional management. Regular physical activity can lower anxiety, improve mood, promote sleep quality, and give an outlet for extra energy or stress. **For adults with autism, consider:**

1. Finding kinds of exercise that correspond with your interests and sensory preferences

2. Incorporating both aerobic activity and strength training

3. Engaging in activities that increase body awareness and coordination, such as yoga or tai chi
4. Using exercise as a type of sensory regulation
5. Considering solo hobbies if team sports feel overwhelming
6. Gradually building up workout routines to avoid burnout

Remember that exercise doesn't have to be intense to be useful. Even brief walks or modest stretching can have positive impacts on emotional well-being.

Integrating sleep, nutrition, and exercise into everyday routines may need some trial and error. It's crucial to pay attention to how different behaviors affect your mental state and modify accordingly. Keep a notebook to track sleep patterns, diet, exercise, and mood to find personal trends and effective solutions.

Lastly, while these lifestyle elements are vital, they should be part of a comprehensive approach to emotional well-being that may also involve therapy, medication (if needed), and other coping mechanisms. By emphasizing sleep, nutrition, and exercise, adults with autism can develop a strong foundation for emotional stability and overall quality of life.

Balancing Work, Relationships, and Personal Time

Achieving a balance between jobs, relationships, and personal leisure is vital for the long-term emotional well-being of adults with autism. This balance can be particularly tough owing to the unique social and sensory experiences associated with autism, but with intentional tactics, it's possible to establish a satisfying and sustainable existence.

In the workplace, consider:

1. Seeking autism-friendly employment environments or accommodations
2. Communicating your demands clearly to employers and colleagues
3. Structuring your workday to include regular breaks and sensory management
4. Using time management techniques to prevent overwhelm
5. Setting clear boundaries between work and personal time

If possible, seek flexible work arrangements that correspond with your natural cycles and sensory needs. This can offer remote work choices, flexible hours, or a calmer environment.

For relationships, focus on:

1. Cultivating a few significant ties rather than a wide social circle

2. Being honest about your social energy limits and desires for alone time
3. Scheduling regular check-ins with friends and family to maintain connections
4. Using communication tools that feel comfortable (e.g., text, email, in-person)
5. Engaging in similar interests as a basis for social interaction

Remember that the quality of relationships frequently matters more than the number. It's alright to have a limited social circle provided those ties are supportive and enjoyable.

Personal time is vital for recharging and pursuing hobbies. Consider:

1. Scheduling aside time for special interests and activities
2. Creating a sensory-friendly personal space at home
3. Engaging in frequent self-care activities

4. Allowing time for solitude and reflection

5. Pursuing personal growth and learning in areas of interest

To effectively balance these areas:

1. Use visual schedules or digital tools to allot time for each life area

2. Regularly examine and alter your balance based on current demands and conditions

3. Practice saying no to obligations that don't correspond with your priorities or well-being

4. Communicate your demands and limitations clearly to others

5. Be flexible and patient with yourself when balance is temporarily interrupted

It's crucial to remember that perfect balance is rarely possible and that needs may alter over time. The goal is to build a sustainable rhythm that fosters general well-being.

For individuals with autism, energy management is often crucial to maintaining equilibrium. Be conscious of activities or situations that drain your energy and those that refill it. Structure your schedule to alternate between these when possible.

Lastly, remember that asking for support is a sign of strength, not weakness. This might involve:

1. Working with a therapist or coach to establish individual balance strategies
2. Joining support groups for adults with autism to exchange experiences and tips
3. Enlisting the aid of friends or family in preserving good boundaries
4. Utilizing assistive technologies or services to handle daily responsibilities

By properly combining employment, relationships, and personal time, adults with autism can develop a lifestyle that supports their specific needs and promotes long-term emotional well-being. This balance offers the framework for personal growth, healthy relationships, and overall life happiness.

Chapter Ten

Continuous Growth and Seeking Support

Setting Realistic Goals for Emotional Regulation

Setting realistic objectives for emotional regulation is a vital stage in the journey of personal growth for persons with autism. These goals provide direction and incentive, while also serving as benchmarks for growth. However, these goals must be adjusted to individual requirements, capabilities, and circumstances to ensure they are realistic and sustainable.

The first step in defining realistic goals is to undertake a thorough self-assessment. This involves focusing on existing emotional control skills, identifying specific obstacles, and acknowledging personal strengths. **Consider questions such as:**

1. What are my most common emotional challenges?
2. In what situations do I struggle most with emotional regulation?
3. What techniques have worked well for me in the past?
4. What are my long-term ambitions for emotional well-being?

This self-reflection provides a framework for developing meaningful and relevant goals.

When developing goals, it's crucial to make them SMART: Specific, Measurable, Achievable, Relevant, and Time-bound. For example, instead of a broad objective like "manage anger better," a SMART goal may be "reduce instances of anger-related meltdowns from twice a week to once a month within the next six months by implementing daily mindfulness practices and weekly therapy sessions."

It's generally useful to split major ambitions into smaller, attainable steps. This strategy, commonly dubbed "chunking," makes the overall aim less intimidating and provides more regular opportunities for accomplishment and positive reinforcement. For instance, if the goal is to promote social-emotional communication, smaller steps can include:

1. Learn three new emotion words each week
2. Practice utilizing "I feel" expressions daily
3. Engage in one social contact per week where you intentionally focus on expressing emotions

Remember that growth in emotional management is rarely linear. There will undoubtedly be setbacks and hurdles along the way. It's crucial to integrate flexibility into your goals and to regard setbacks as learning opportunities rather than failures.

Regularly assessing and changing goals is vital. Set aside time every few months to monitor progress, acknowledge wins (no matter how minor), and alter goals as appropriate. This constant approach guarantees that your goals remain relevant and motivating.

Consider involving a trustworthy friend, family member, or therapist in the goal-setting process. They can provide essential outside perspectives and support. They might also help uncover goals that you may not have considered.

It's also vital to develop goals that focus on the process of emotional control, not just the end. For example, a goal can be to "practice deep breathing exercises for five minutes each day," rather than "never have a meltdown again." Process-oriented goals reflect the continuing nature of emotional regulation and provide a sense of accomplishment in the day-to-day work of personal growth.

Lastly, remember to develop goals that recognize and appreciate your autistic identity. The purpose is not to disguise or suppress autistic tendencies, but to build emotional regulation skills that enhance your quality of life while respecting your neurodiversity.

By creating realistic, customized objectives for emotional regulation, adults with autism can develop a roadmap for continuing growth and improvement in their emotional well-being. This proactive approach helps individuals to take control of their emotional experiences and work towards a more balanced and meaningful existence.

When and How to Seek Professional Support

Seeking professional support is a critical element of emotional regulation and overall well-being for persons with autism. Recognizing when to seek help and understanding how to receive suitable support can dramatically boost the quality of life and stimulate personal growth.

Knowing when to seek professional guidance is the first step. **Some signals that it might be time to visit a professional include:**

1. Persistent sensations of anxiety, despair, or emotional overwhelm
2. Difficulty managing everyday responsibilities due to emotional problems
3. Increased frequency or intensity of meltdowns or shutdowns
4. Struggles with work, relationships, or self-care

5. Development of hazardous coping methods (e.g., substance abuse, self-harm)

6. Feeling trapped or unable to make progress in personal growth

7. Experiencing a huge life shift or loss

8. Desiring to understand oneself better or to build new coping strategies

It's crucial to emphasize that one doesn't need to be in crisis to benefit from expert support. Regular check-ins with a mental health practitioner can be a proactive way to sustain emotional well-being.

When it comes to how to seek support, the process might seem onerous, especially for adults with autism who can find navigating healthcare institutions problematic. **Here are some steps to consider:**

1. Research professionals who specialize in adult autism. Look for psychologists, psychiatrists, or therapists with experience in this field. Online

directories, autism organizations, and referrals from trusted healthcare practitioners can be useful starting places.

2. Consider the type of help needed. This could include individual therapy, group therapy, skills training, medication management, or a mix of these.

3. Prepare for the initial appointment. Write down worries, questions, and goals. Consider providing a list of existing techniques, both productive and ineffective.

4. Be upfront about autism during the initial encounter. If the expert isn't already specialized in autism, educate them about personal experiences and demands.

5. Assess the fit with the professional. It's normal to try different therapists or tactics to find the appropriate match. Look for someone who respects

autistic identity and approaches help from a neurodiversity-affirming perspective.

6. Explore different therapeutic modalities. Cognitive Behavioral Therapy (CBT), Dialectical Behavior Therapy (DBT), and mindfulness-based therapies have demonstrated advantages for many adults with autism.

7. Consider telemedicine options if in-person appointments are hard due to sensory or social concerns.

8. Look into support groups for adults with autism. These can give significant peer assistance alongside professional help.

9. Investigate potential financial help or insurance coverage for mental health care.

10. Be patient with the procedure. Building a therapy relationship and witnessing success takes time.

Remember that seeking professional support is a show of strength, not weakness. It indicates a dedication to personal improvement and well-being. Many adults with autism discover that professional support offers them fresh insights, techniques, and views that dramatically improve their quality of life.

By understanding when and how to seek professional care, adults with autism can access vital resources for emotional control and overall mental health. This proactive approach to well-being can lead to enhanced self-understanding, better-coping abilities, and a more rewarding life experience.

Self-Advocacy and Educating Others About Your Emotional Needs

Self-advocacy and teaching people about one's emotional needs are key skills for adults with autism. These qualities empower individuals to establish supportive surroundings, foster understanding relationships, and guarantee that their unique needs are recognized and honored.

Self-advocacy in the context of emotional needs involves:

1. Developing self-awareness: Understand your emotional patterns, triggers, and coping techniques. This self-knowledge is the foundation of effective self-advocacy.

2. Communicating needs clearly: Learn to articulate your emotional requirements in a direct, explicit

manner. This can require explaining how specific places or circumstances influence you emotionally.

3. Setting boundaries: Establish and maintain appropriate boundaries that safeguard your emotional well-being. This could involve minimizing exposure to overstimulating situations or scheduling regular alone time.

4. Requesting accommodations: Whether in the workplace or social contexts, don't hesitate to ask for acceptable accommodations that help your emotional regulation.

5. Standing up for your rights: Familiarize yourself with applicable disability laws and rights. Be prepared to assert these rights as required.

6. Practicing assertiveness: Develop the ability to express your opinions, feelings, and needs boldly and politely.

Educating others about your emotional needs as an adult with autism is an ongoing effort that demands patience and persistence. **Here are several strategies:**

1. Choose the correct time and place: Select a peaceful moment for critical chats about your needs, preferably in a comfortable location.

2. Use precise, concrete language: Avoid ambiguity. Provide detailed instances of your experiences and needs.

3. Utilize visual aids: If helpful, utilize diagrams, charts, or written information to augment your remarks.

4. Share resources: Provide reputable articles, books, or videos regarding autism and emotional regulation to assist people in comprehending your perspective.

5. Be open to questions: Encourage others to ask inquiries. This encourages understanding and shows your willingness to engage in discourse.

6. Explain the 'why' behind your needs: Help others comprehend the reasoning behind your needs or behaviors. For example, explain how some sensory experiences can contribute to emotional excess.

7. Offer solutions: When describing issues, also suggest alternative solutions or accommodations that could help.

8. Be patient: Remember that comprehending may take time. Be prepared to review issues and provide reminders as needed.

9. Lead by example: Model the kind of understanding and respect you desire to receive from others.

10. Connect with the universal: While expressing your specific demands, also emphasize parallels in emotional experiences that others might relate to.

It's crucial to realize that you're not compelled to educate everyone about your emotional needs. Choose to share with those who play major roles in your life and in situations where understanding is crucial for your well-being.

Self-advocacy and education are powerful tools for creating a more inclusive and understanding environment. By effectively conveying your emotional needs and educating people about the autistic experience, you not only improve your quality of life but also contribute to wider knowledge and acceptance of neurodiversity in society.

These skills may take time to learn, and it's okay to start modestly. Each step taken in self-advocacy and education is a step towards a more supportive and understanding world for adults with autism.

Printed in Great Britain
by Amazon